Ask me

Can lizards disappear?

Reptiles and Birds

Contents

2

What has scaly skin?

Crocodiles, tortoises, lizards and snakes all have scaly skin, and they are all reptiles. Their skin is also dry and very tough. Reptiles have a skeleton inside their bodies, and a backbone. All reptiles are cold-blooded. This means they need to sunbathe each morning to warm up. Most reptiles also lay their eggs on dry land.

↑ Wet amphibians

Frogs and toads have skeletons, lay eggs, and are cold-blooded, but they're not reptiles. They are amphibians, which means that their skin is moist, and not dry and scaly.

Crocodile

Where do reptiles live?

Python

Most lizards and snakes live on land, and most turtles and crocodiles live in water. Reptiles, like this shovel-snouted lizard, live in the hot desert. To keep cool, the lizard holds two legs up in the air. Then, it switches legs.

Giant tortoise

Iguana

? True or false

Reptiles were the first creatures to roam the Earth.

True. But they didn't look like the reptiles we see today. Dinosaurs were the first reptiles to live on Earth a very long time ago.

Can lizards disappear?

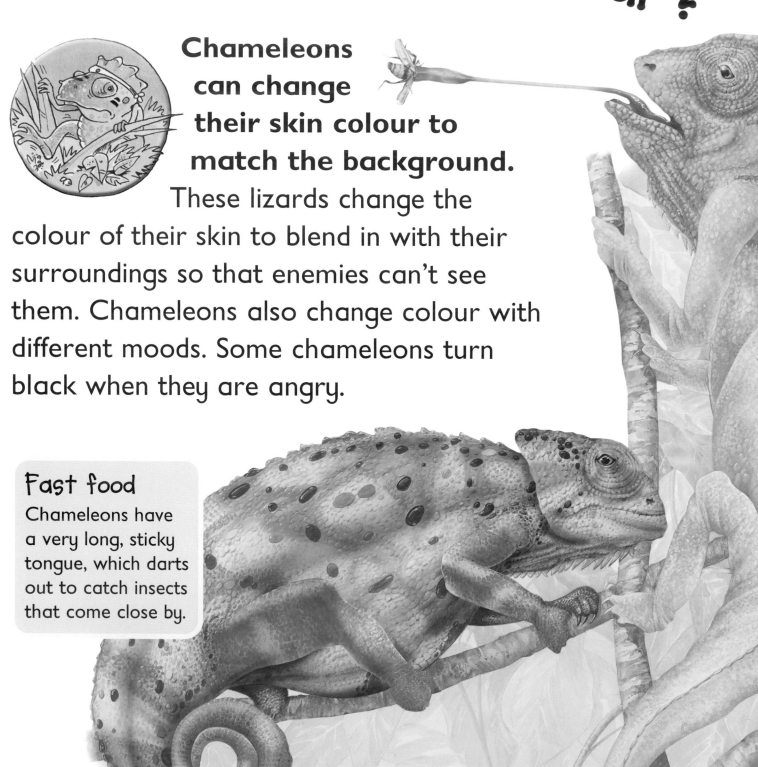

Chameleons can change their skin colour to match the background. These lizards change the colour of their skin to blend in with their surroundings so that enemies can't see them. Chameleons also change colour with different moods. Some chameleons turn black when they are angry.

Fast food
Chameleons have a very long, sticky tongue, which darts out to catch insects that come close by.

6

Why do lizards change their skin?

Lizards and snakes grow too big for their skin, just as we grow too big for our clothes. When this happens, the old, tight skin peels off and there's a shiny new skin underneath.

← Sneaky sand snake
The desert adder is the same colour as the sand. It buries itself in the sand with only its eyes and horns sticking out.

Which reptiles wear armour?

Turtles, tortoises and terrapins have a hard shell built onto their skeleton that's like a suit of armour. The shell is made of two pieces, a top and a bottom, with openings for the head, legs and tail.

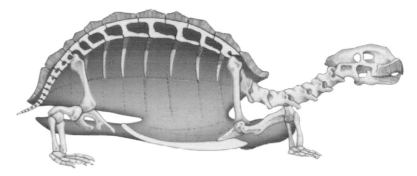

Who has two tongues?

Some lizards and snakes have a tongue with a forked end, but they have only one tongue. In fact, snakes and forked-tongue lizards use their tongue like a nose – to smell with! They flick their tongue in and out of their mouth all the time to pick up smells around them.

Which snakes can see in the dark?

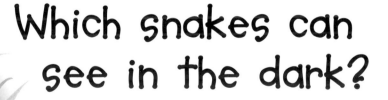

Pit vipers hunt at night, when it is dark. Next to each eye they have a little hollow that can feel the heat waves given off by other animals. With this, they can 'see' animals in darkness.

8

Komodo dragon

? True or false

There's a kind of reptile alive today that lived with dinosaurs.

True. Tuataras have been on Earth for millions of years, and they haven't changed much in that time. Tuataras have a third eye that helps them to tell when it's light or dark.

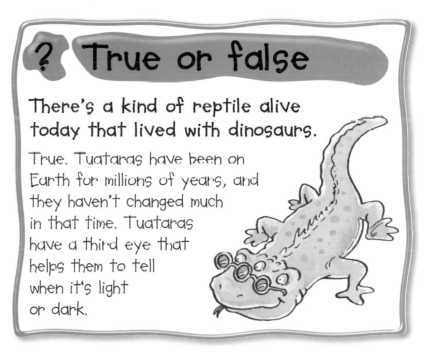

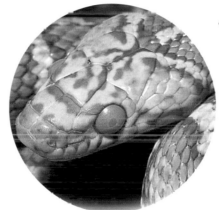

← Snake glasses
Snakes have no eyelids to protect their eyes. Instead, they have a see-through disk that covers and protects each eye.

Who has swivel eyes?

The chameleon can make each eye swivel in different directions. This means it can make one eye look to the front, while the other eye looks to the back. It can see where it's going and where it's been at the same time! Chameleons may have excellent eyesight, but their hearing is very poor.

Do snakes have teeth?

Yes, snakes have teeth, but they do not use them for chewing. Snakes have very small, sharp teeth. Their teeth point backwards, so the snake cannot chew with them. Instead, snakes use their teeth to grip their prey. Most snakes swallow their food whole. Muscles in the body help to push the food through the snake's body.

Which reptiles share a feast?

When a crocodile catches a big animal, others nearby join in the feast. This is because a single crocodile can't tear up a large animal by itself.

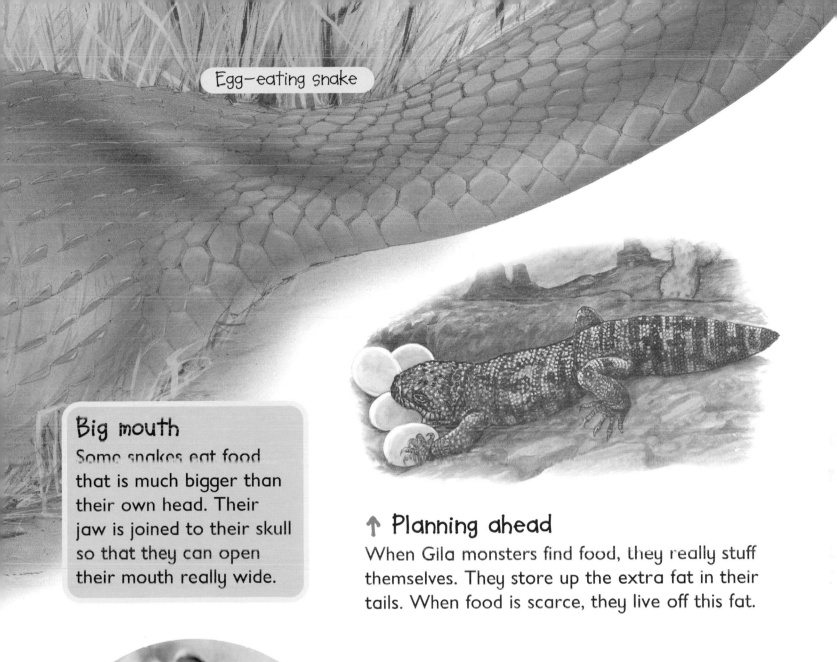

Egg-eating snake

Big mouth

Some snakes eat food that is much bigger than their own head. Their jaw is joined to their skull so that they can open their mouth really wide.

↑ Planning ahead

When Gila monsters find food, they really stuff themselves. They store up the extra fat in their tails. When food is scarce, they live off this fat.

Which snake fishes?

The tentacled snake, which is a water snake. As it swims on the riverbed, the two tentacles on its snout wave in the water like wriggly worms. When a fish comes close, attracted by the 'worms', it is snatched up and eaten by the snake.

Who lives in the sea?

Turtles spend most of their lives in the sea. Some swim halfway around the world to lay their eggs, then swim all the way back again. Like all reptiles, turtles lay their eggs on dry land. They swim to a beach and lay their eggs, then go back to the sea.

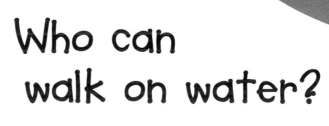

Who can walk on water?

The tiny basilisk lizard can walk on water, but it has to move fast. The lizard can cross a pond without sinking if it runs. The lizard runs upright like this when it's being chased.

12

Which snake seems to fly?

Tree snakes can glide through the air. These snakes live high in the treetops. To move around, they push themselves up into the air. They make their body flat to glide more easily.

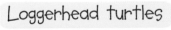
Loggerhead turtles

Do you know?

1. Is a turtle a reptile?
2. Can a lizard walk on water?

Answers: 1. Yes, even though it spends most of its life in water. 2. Yes, the basilisk lizard.

→ **It's a stick-up**
Geckos can walk up walls and across the ceiling. They have little scales on their feet that act like suction pads. These keep the gecko firmly stuck to the wall.

Who has a frilly collar?

The frilled lizard has a huge, frilly collar! It raises the collar to scare away enemies. When an enemy comes close, the lizard sticks out the frilly flaps of skin attached to its neck. This makes it look much bigger and scarier than it really is. It also opens its mouth wide and hisses.

← **Little squirt**
The horned lizard has a nasty way of scaring off enemies. It squirts jets of blood out of its eyes!

Which lizard has a scary tongue?

The blue-tongued skink has a fat blue tongue! When the skink is threatened, it puffs up its body to make itself look much bigger than it is. It then sticks out its large blue tongue at the enemy.

← End of the tail

Some lizards, like this tree skink, can make their tails drop off when they are attacked. The dropped tail keeps moving and is watched by the enemy while the lizard escapes. The lizard grows a new tail.

Which snake spits?

The spitting cobra. If the cobra is attacked, it spits two fine sprays of poison at its enemy. It usually tries to spit into the eyes of the enemy. The poison blinds the attacker for a while, and the cobra has time to get away.

Who is supermum?

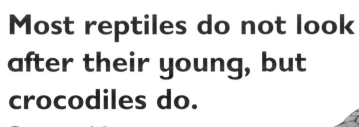

Most reptiles do not look after their young, but crocodiles do. Crocodiles cover their eggs with soil and grass to keep them warm and also to hide them from enemies. When the babies hatch, the mother gently carries them in her mouth to the water.

Who lays the most eggs?

Sea turtles lay at least 100 eggs. The green turtle can lay as many as 1000 eggs in different places.

Do turtles build nests?

No, female turtles dig holes in the beach where they lay their eggs. When the eggs hatch, the tiny turtles race down the beach to the sea. They have to be quick so they're not caught by gulls and lizards.

↑ Calling mum
Baby crocodiles tap the shells of their eggs to call their mum when they are ready to hatch. She then helps them out of their eggs.

? True or false

Reptile eggs are like bird eggs.

False. Most reptile eggs have a tough, leathery shell to keep the baby inside safe. Bird eggshells are thin and easily broken. Some geckos lay eggs that are more like a bird's eggs.

Which animals have wings?

Birds have wings, and birds are animals. Nearly all birds have feathers to help them fly and to keep them warm. All birds have beaks instead of mouths, and they have wings instead of front legs — and all birds lay eggs.

↑ Beautiful bird
The quetzal of South America has beautiful, long, green tail feathers. The ancient Maya and Aztec people who lived hundreds of years ago thought the bird was a god.

Bright birds
Some birds have very colourful feathers. These macaws are a type of parrot.

→ Bird bed

The wandering albatross has a bigger wingspan than any other bird – 3 metres (10 feet) across. You could easily lie down on its outstretched wings!

↑ Truly tiny

The smallest bird is the bee hummingbird. It is only as long as a person's thumb.

Can all birds fly?

No, even though all birds have wings. Ostriches and emus can't fly, but they have strong legs so they can run fast. Penguins can't fly, either, but they're great swimmers.

Who is king of the sky?

Eagles are some of the biggest and strongest birds that fly. Eagles hunt during the day and can spot the smallest movement on the ground below. They have a sharp beak and strong talons to grab their prey. Eagles catch fish and small animals.

Bald eagle

Which birds travel the most?

Arctic terns travel amazing distances and never get lost. They breed in the Arctic, but when winter begins, they travel to the opposite side of the world. This journey is called migration.

→ Nosy hunter

Kiwis are birds that can't fly. They live in New Zealand. They sniff out their favourite food, worms, using nostrils on the tip of their beak.

Who flies at night?

Most owls sleep during the day and hunt at night. Their excellent hearing and eyesight mean they can hunt and catch even the smallest animal when it's dark.

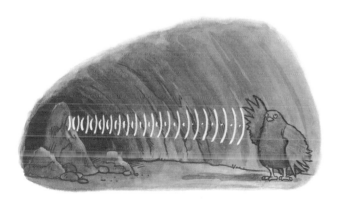

↑ Being noisy

Making little noises helps some birds to find their way around in dark caves.

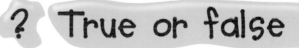

? True or false

Penguins shut their eyes underwater.

False. Penguins do not have eyelids like you do. But they do need to protect their eyes from the freezing, salty wind and water, so they have see-through eyelids that act like goggles.

Why is the flamingo pink?

The flamingo gets its pink colour from its food. It eats pink shrimps. If it stops eating pink shrimps, it turns a greyish-white colour. A flamingo's beak is full of tiny holes. It uses its beak like a sieve, to catch the small shrimps when it takes a gulp of water.

Which bird fishes under an umbrella?

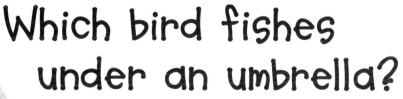

Many herons spread their wings like an umbrella when they hunt. They tuck in their head and wait. Soon a fish swims into the shady water and is caught by the heron.

Which bird stores food?

The acorn woodpecker finds acorns during the autumn and stores them in oak trees. It drills lots of small holes in the bark of the tree, just the right size for an acorn to fit. This way the woodpecker has enough food stored to last all year.

↑ Watch out!

Crows sit on the fences next to roads. They watch carefully for any animals that get run over and eat the remains.

↓ A helping beak

Ox-peckers help big animals to get rid of their nits. They sit on animals, like giraffes, and eat the tiny insects that live in the animals' fur.

Do you know?

1. What makes a flamingo pink?
2. What do ox-peckers eat?

Answers: 1. The food it eats. 2. The tiny insects that live on big animals.

Why do turkeys go red?

When male wild turkeys have a fight, the flap of skin on their neck changes colour from purply red to bright red. The male whose flap is the biggest and reddest is usually the strongest, and the other turkeys leave him alone. The flap of skin is called a wattle.

Who eats leftovers?

Vultures eat what is left over from another animal's meal. Vultures don't hunt and kill food for themselves. Some vultures steal and eat bird eggs.

Who has four eyes?

The sun bittern has markings on its wings that look like scary eyes. It shows these eyes if it is about to be attacked. The enemy thinks the eyes belong to a bigger animal and runs.

↑ Big bully
The frigate bird does not always bother finding its own food. Instead, it will swoop down to attack a seabird with a fish in its beak and snatch the fish for itself.

? True or false

A swan has very strong wings.

True. Swans have very powerful wings. If they are threatened, they attack with their huge wings spread out. Their wings are so strong they can break a person's arm. They also have a strong neck and beak.

Who has blue feet?

A male blue-footed booby.
The male booby performs a special dance to attract females. Keeping the rest of his body very still, the bird slowly raises first his right foot, and then his left foot. He does this so the female notices his bright blue feet!

↑ Booming bird
The lyrebird is very good at imitating other sounds. He can make noises such as car horns and the sound of a mobile phone ringing.

26

Which bird loves the colour blue?

Male blue bowerbirds collect bits of blue treasure to attract a female. They make arches, or bowers, out of twigs or grasses. In front of this, they place all the blue things they have found, such as petals, shells and berries, and objects such as bottletops.

Quick stopover

Boobies spend most of their time at sea. They only come onto land to find a mate and raise their young.

Which birds sing a duet?

Pairs of tawny owls sing together to keep track of where they are in the dark. They reply to each other so quickly that the sound seems to come from one bird.

Who has a messy nest?

A stork's nest is usually a mess. Storks make a nest at the top of a tree, but in towns they build nests on chimney tops. The nest is a messy collection of twigs. Storks stay together for life and will come back to the same nest year after year.

Who traps his mate in a tree?

The red-billed hornbill traps his mate in a hole in a tree trunk. He builds a door of mud but leaves a tiny gap to pass food to her. This is so enemies can't reach her or the eggs.

Which birds live in apartments?

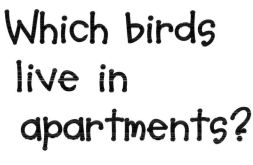

Sociable weaver birds live in a giant nest like an apartment block. The huge nest is made from dried grasses. The nest hangs from the branch of a tree and has lots of spaces for pairs of birds and their chicks.

↑ Spit and feathers

Swifts and swallows have super strong spit! They use it to stick together dropped feathers and grass to make their nests.

? True or false

Some birds line their nests with their own feathers.

True. Some birds pull feathers from their chests to line their nests. House wrens sometimes use cast-off snake skins for their nests, and honey-eaters take hair from people's heads!

Who has a foot nest?

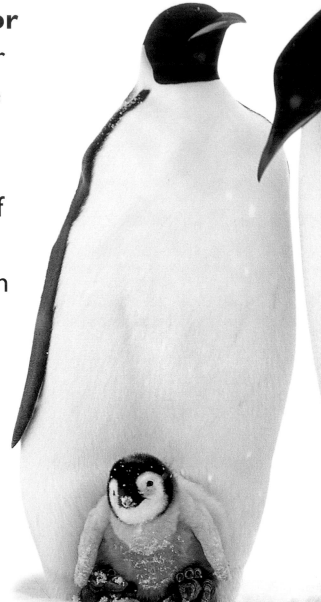

The baby emperor penguin. Emperor penguins live in the Antarctic where it's freezing cold. There are no twigs to build a nest, and if the egg was laid on the ground, it would freeze. So the egg is kept on the father's feet until it hatches, while the mother finds food. Parents take turns keeping the chick on their feet until it is about two months old.

← Cooling shower
A stork in Australia carries water in its beak to its nest. It spits the water onto the eggs to cool them.

Which chicks go to a nursery?

The eider duck leaves her ducklings in a nursery. The nanny bird takes care of as many as 30 ducklings.

Who has fingers?

Hoatzin chicks have two claw-like fingers on each wing. The chick uses these to clamber over trees and to climb back into its nest if it falls out of the tree.

→ **Follow me**
Plovers lay their eggs on the ground. If an enemy appears, the bird pretends to have a broken wing, so the enemy follows it.

Index

This edition published in 2007
Reprinted in 2008
The Southwestern Company UK Ltd
Goldsmiths House, Broad Plain, Bristol BS2 0JP
© Southwestern Company 2002, 2005

British Library Cataloguing-in-Publication Data
A catalogue record for this book is available from the British Library

ISBN 978-0-87197-533-1

SW Southwestern

Produced by Miles Kelly Publishing Ltd
Bardfield Centre, Great Bardfield, Essex CM7 4SL, UK

Publishing Director: Anne Marshall
Designer: Warris Kidwai

Printed in China

Project Director, UK: Fiona Greenland
Editorial Director: Mary Cummings
Managing Editor: Judy Jackson
Copy Editor: Carolyn King
Production Manager: Powell Ropp
Digital Prepress Coordinator: Donna Bailey

The publishers would like to thank the following artists whose work appears in this book: John Butler,
Steve Caldwell, Jim Channell, Andrew Clark, Mark Davis, Kuo Kang Chen, Andrew Clark, Peter Dennis,
Heather Dickinson, Richard Draper, James Field, Nicholas Forder, Chris Forsey, Mike Foster/Maltings
Partnership, Terry Gabbey, Alan Hancocks, Richard Hook, John James, Emma Jones, Tony Kenyon, Aziz Khan,
Sue King/SGA, Kevin Maddison, Janos Marffy, Debbie Meekcoms, Helen Parsley, Rachel Philips, Jane Pickering,
Neil Reid, Terry Riley, Pete Roberts, Steve Roberts, Peter Sarson, Martin Sanders, Mike Saunders, Sarah Smith,
Studio Galante, Rudi Vizi, Mike White, Paul Williams, Peter Wilks.